This book is dedicated to my
dear prayer warriors near and far
to whom I am very grateful.

POEMS

Foreword..............................ix
SPIRITUAL RENEWAL..............2

Struggle on, Fall and Rise Up
Lord, Mold Me in Your Ovens
My Heart Has It All
Bury the Past. Change the Future.
New Year 2020
No Grand Resolutions in 2021
Daily Living.
The Meeting Place
The Thief's Clean-Out

INTERFACE WITH GOD........11

Lord, I Will Walk with Thee
The Daily Grind
Cancer's Fist Punch
Work of Art
The Potter

SELF-INTROSPECTION..........16

Waiting
Being Still.
A New Me.
Your Own Kind of beautiful

FAITH...........................19

He Renews Me
Leaving

The Reality of God
He Worketh
Hope

MYSTERY 23

Sacred Idleness
Pie in the Sky
Journaling

MY FATE WITH CANCER . 26

Buried In My Genetic Past
Fears Dispel. Doubts Scatter.

LIFE'S CHALLENGE 28

The Firmament
The Crucible
The Gift
Tomorrow Today
The Song Of the Lion
Let the Kindness Out
The Journeys and Destinations
Time Zones
Bask in the Sun
Get Off the Wheel
Turmoil
The Light of the World
Laddering and Snaking
The Flight of the Kite

REFLECTIONS

My Cancer Recovery Mission Statement

SCRIPTURE..43

So they weren't able to enter due to their disbelief
Come Unto Me All Ye That Labour
The Exodus 35:30-31
Mocking Words
You Yourselves Give Them Something to Eat
He Would Go to Lonely Places
The Spirit of the Lord Is Upon Me
He Must Increase, I Must Decrease.
This Is My Son With Whom I Am Pleased
The Sabbath Was Made For Man
Faith, If It Hath Not Works, Is Dead
Blessed Are The Poor In Spirit
The Beatitude That Stands Out For Me
Christmas Is Incarnation
He Will Bring Down Your Fortified Walls

FAITH...54

Matt. 28:31 My Favourite Bible Account
Courage. It is I.
The One Who Calls You Is Faithful
A Gracious Woman Gains Respect
Fear Not

Be Still and Know I am God
Be a River, Not a Reservoir of God's Mercy.
Daughter, Your Faith Has Made You Well
Matthew 14 :29

SELF-INTROSPECTION...................61

Let Old Acquaintance Be Forgot
Thank You For Loving Me
I Am Weak

MYSTERY..............................63
In the Silence
Being Still
Dream
Be the Rainbow in Someone's Cloud
Created in His Image

TRIAL AND SUFFERING...............67

My Thin Place
The Chosen
Trust and Submission
My Gethsemane
Being in Darkness

INTERFACE WITH GOD.............71

Thank You Father
A Prayer
I am the Lord's YoYo
The Dislodged Log
I Am Like Broken Pottery

Forgiveness Ends Hate
May Day
Contentment
Do What You Can With What You Have
Shove It In and Let It Go.
Faith is Lifelong
Restore My Spirit, Lord
Listening to God
O Wondrous Creator

Acknowledgements......................81

About the Author.......................85

Take off your shoes.....................87

A note from the author

These are verses from my head and heart. I am in waiting. I don't know for what. A calling perhaps? I dreamed of this and in my waking, actually saw the words CREATE on no less a background than a wall.

This is my recovery time. My body has weary bones and muscles. My mind and soul is a blank. My strength is at an ebb. But I wait for His refreshing dew to nourish my spirit. I wait for His shoes of iron and brass to strengthen my steps.

These steps that I shall take towards...WHAT GOAL? WHAT MISSION? But till it is made known to me, I CREATE: crotchet, sew, knit, work with craft, cook...

"To this end, I strenuously contend with all the energy which Christ so powerfully works in me." Colossians 1:29.

Teresa

FOREWORD

Way back in 1970, when I first met Teresa on the village green sometime in May, I was smitten and I invited her to join me in a Christian youth sodality group that was engaged in apostolic work. But it was then, that I saw in Teresa an inherent talent in drama when she played a lead role in William Saroyan's "Hello Out There." Later, we got on like a house on fire and four months later I wrote her "My song in September." That was a piece of modern verse with which I told her we were created to make a life together.

    Teresa graduated in the Sciences a couple of years later but had to abandon earlier plans of going to medical school. Yet, in some of her love letters, I sensed her bent for verse. She, of course, preferred to hide that light under a bushel.

    We've had a great life together and earlier this year celebrated a golden wedding with our three kids Golda, Aaron and Esther; their spouses Stephen, Kristina and Marc and seven grandkids: Liam, Elliot, Nathaniel, Gabriel, Evangeline, Edith and Agnes.

But the last seven years tells a grim story. On July 8, 2018, a ton of bricks had come down on us when a doctor walked into Teresa's hospital room and said apologetically: "I am sorry, I don't have good news for you. Radiology tells us you've got cancer."

These years could have been traumatic for us. But Teresa is a woman of faith and did not seem to despair. Yet in her private moments, she would pick up the phone and comfort others living with cancer bringing hope to all of those she connected with.

In those private moments she also would grab pieces of paper and journal her thoughts, her conversations with God, reflections on scriptural verse and feed her hunger for a spiritual renewal. She did this in verse and in scripture reflections, reviving a latent talent.

In this collection of verse and reflections, Teresa dwells on suffering and tribulation; the glorious gift of God's mercy and compassion; the mystery around silence; of walking with Jesus in faith, in trust and submission; embracing the struggle of falling and rising again; of getting off the wheel; burying the past; stepping in as the rainbow in someone's cloud and in so doing healing our Gethsemane.

It is my hope that these poems and reflections will inspire and lift you up and bring you the joy you seek.

Robin Arthur
Author of *Science and the God Elusion*

BOOK 1

POEMS
Veracity in Verse

Who is going to read these pages?
Who will browse these words
That took me ages?
Who will ponder on my meaning?
Or wonder about the feeling?
Then with every word that didn't fit in
Will pain hurt when it's unwritten

SPIRITUAL RENEWAL

STRUGGLE ON, FALL AND RISE UP

This day is your tomorrow
Use it as a gift
Do not dwell on the sorrow
As through glass sand will sift.
There's no time for regrets,
Those are lessons learned.
Use them well as your tenets
When tables are turned.
Through it all He has your back
And He knows it all....
How you try to change your life
Struggle on, get up and fall.

LORD, MOLD ME IN YOUR OVENS AGAIN

May I be the person you created, I prayed.
You changed and molded me and I resisted.
It must have been really hard on You.
But I am glad You insisted.

I didn't understand Your vision, Your love.

But this time you broke the old mold.

Cracks may have appeared to Your divine gaze
And a new me began to unfold,

All broken, I'm back on your wheel.
I hope I'm getting the rough edges cleaned
Smoothed by your loving hands.
I'm getting a sturdy structure of steel
All ready for your shape
and oven fires again.

MY HEART HAS IT ALL!

It's all in my head.
The thoughts you may never know.
The buzz, the grit on which I have fed
And with my going will go.

It's all in my body.
The strength that compels the mind.
The pain, the aches, the rest as well, Lordy,
That I occasionally find.

It's all in my spirit
The faith that I show the world.
The joy, the belief, the happiness in it
That the Lord has revealed and unfurled.

But my heart really has it all.
A stranger, family or friend
Who holds me up, lifts me when I fall.
And stamps indelibly, a loving brand.

BURY THE PAST
CHANGE THE FUTURE

It's hard to remember
When it's December
What one has done
For heaven to be won
Then you look back and think
And your heart might sink
Over the actions of the past
And the memory that lasts
But think of them, you must
If the future you trust
A future of no repeat,

Of the errors you could not beat
Your courage you shouldn't lack
But live and learn from looking back.
The hours go by in swiftness
Daylight chasing away dark
Night slips into the morning
When we hear songs of the lark.

NEW YEAR 2020

I pulled in the New Year last night.
It didn't want to come.
I sat it down while it lost its fight
And questions I asked it some.

It groans and moans and trembles
And talks of things to come
About storms and floods and rumbles
How would I take it all?

I asked what about the others,
The births, the laughter, the joys
The big plans, eventful dates, a mixed bag
Out from the mist and fog.

I said: "Don't you worry about me
I sure do appreciate your concern.
You have my word, you see.
And my faith and spirit and love.

You are my gift from Him
And I want you to stay
Whatever he has packed into you
I will willingly take.

So, 2020 my dear friend
Stay and unfold yourself.
I'll treat you well, I will muster strength
To deal with all you bring.

I'll ask for a clean heart
And to renew my spirit each day
With shoes of iron and helping hands
That have used His word to pray.

No tears unless for joy
Very little drama per day
Count to ten as a ploy
Before gently, words do say.

So, let's welcome you well
Stay for a year and let's do a deal.
I promise to use you and tell the world
That you sure came with His seal.

So are we ready, then, to start each day
In love and prayer we daily unfold
An open mind, and let's say
Aim for a heart of gold

NO GRAND RESOLUTIONS
in 2021

Be calm. Talk gently.
Pray. Love. Listen.
Give of myself, my kindness to others.
Talk straight. Say what I mean
And mean what I say. No subterfuge.
But wait. Check my words.
Get rid of the resentment
Most of all, build up faith.
And always remember
That I have Jesus by my side.
Around me, in me and I belong to Him.
2020 over and out.

DAILY LIVING

I want to live with the Spirit
While I walk with the Lord
Giving thanks to the Creator
The face of God.

Be clothed in His grace
With God in my Heart
Be bathed in the water
And make a fresh start.

There's the mystery of life
That I cannot solve
But live it I can
With love and resolve.

I can wake up with prayer
With a whole, clean heart.
And a renewed spirit
To do my part.

No tag to my name.
But to just walk in love
Understanding my fellowman
Will be my gift from above

THE MEETING PLACE

A square, fenced-off area
Under a giant tree,
Is where we usually sit.
Creator, Lord, the Spirit and me.

At the end of my day
I wander gently
And always feel the glow
Of love breathing my way.

Today, ah! Tonight, the gate is shut.
It's my day. I was expected.
My heart hammers.
Am I late?

In my little picket-fenced spot
Under the darkening sky
It's always bright.
There I am at peace. I fear not.

THE THIEF"S CLEAN-OUT

He comes. He rummages.
He ruffles. He takes.
He leaves behind breakages
What a mess he makes.

To yourself be a thief.
Go in with intent to steal.
All your inner closets you heave
And set out to heal.

Take the precious parts of you
And hold them safe to keep
Bundle the nasty, bad you do.
So ill you shouldn't reap.

You'll have to clean out the mess
Never looking back, rid the bad.
And like the thief, hug the rest
Of the good and pure you always had.

INTERFACE WITH GOD

LORD I WILL
WALK WITH THEE

I come up to take a breath
In between the years
Keeping my head above the tears
As drowning becomes a threat.
I know who holds my hand
As I struggle to stay on the water
He was there with me on the day
I said Lord I will walk with Thee.
Not on solid ground anymore
My feet have been wet
But with You I see the distant shore
While I smile in happy optimism
That to life here, there must be more
Your earth is beautiful.
Your created ones should be sublime
I try to see that ethereal pull
Of my fellows who feel like they're mine.
Mine to love, gifted to me by You.
I look out for them with a heart that's true.
But sometimes dear Lord,
After 72 years of living
I can get so sad and weary
Lord, walk with me.

The Daily Grind

From sunrise to sunset and beyond
I know I am in your care
Help me with joy
My burdens to bear.

Let my heart sing
As my spirit bubbles
Let me touch everything
Not be touched by troubles

From dawn to dusk
As the hours speed
And I attempt each task,
Please, my spirit I need.

No imagined hurts or ego
Nor with pride be seen
But presumptions I let go
With heart renewed and clean.

CANCER'S FIST PUNCH

I used to have a bucket list
And nothing got ticked
When cancer punched me with its fist
I thought I was truly licked!!

Not so fast, my friend...
My bucket list has a hole
All it needs is a little mend
Which is quite a consuming goal.

So, I called on the Lord
And I called on kith and kin
The friends came in a crowd
And heaven's gate they broke in.

I'm keeping my usual cool
And lifting my spirit in cheer.
Lord, I know you're with me
So why should I fear?

WORK
OF ART

Lord, I am your work
You are the potter
I am the clay
Am I not finished yet?
A work in progress, I see.
You need time, I acknowledge.
Shape me, make me
But when will I be finished?
By myself I'm unable.
I need all Your graces
To fulfill the plan on the table.
Of Your masterpiece, any traces?
Help me understand
Why I didn't meet your plan
Surely, I was meant to be
Better than what I am?
You're still working, Lord
On a really good me.
I must be a piece of art
That only you can see?
Others can't make me out
Sugar and spice not nice?
I had a super start
What's happening with Your art?

THE POTTER

Countless times O Lord
Have you molded the clay.
Each crack mended but
Why should imperfection stay?

Reshaped, restructured
almost to the DNA!
Chances granted to me
As numerous as the stars..
To choose and start again,
with another slap of clay

Yet, no lessons learnt,
With every turn of the wheel
I have resisted.
And now that's how I feel.

But with patience and love
You redeemed me,
I am the work of Your hands.
Lord, you know I love thee.

SELF INTROSPECTION

WAITING

What does one do with an awesome gift?
What do I do with the gift of faith?
Hold it close to treasure and wait?
Or be still and do not shift?

But that was not how you created me.
I was born a tiny stick of dynamite.
I have been smoldering, the flame burning
and dimming over the years.

I've tried being still,
Being fluid, being calm.
Just being who I think I am.
I am here, Lord. Speak.

BEING STILL...

There is a rock on the bank.
It doesn't blink.
There is water in the stream.
It doesn't stop.

The years go by and by
The rock not blinking;
The water not stopping.
The status quo.
The sun's, moon's, stars' endless cycle.
The rock slows the flow.
The water smooths the rock.
The gravel in the earth
Is where the water seeped.
Both have lived and loved.

A NEW ME

Dear Lord as you can see
I'm somewhat the same old me
Going which, what, every way
From one day to another day.

I'm hoping to slowly change
A new me for the old exchange
Hope to do it slowly, gently
And look at life quite differently.

I'm going to, firstly, stop and think
Halt myself right on the brink
Of voicing an opinion or a thought
In a tangled web not be caught.

I want to use every moment in time
To not just write some futile rhyme
But to connect with family and friends
Coz on God and them my life depends.

I see myself evolving slowly
But not completely wholly.
We'll keep the kindness, dump the haste
To listen more and time not waste.

YOU ARE YOUR OWN BEAUTIFUL

Your ears are open to pleas
And your heart whispers a hope
Everyone you appease
Gracefully trying to cope.

You are your own beautiful
While you view life from the top
Obey and are dutiful
Yet command tear drops to stop.

Aurem cordis, occoli cordi
With ears and eyes of your heart
Tuned with everyone's story
Beauty, love never apart.

FAITH

HE RENEWS ME

The sea is calm.
I am holding His hand,
He's holding my arm
It feels like a band
Around my soul
There is a glow
Which cocoons fully
And whole.
He renews me again and again.
Each time, more strong I grow in grace
And grounded.
I know...Oh I know
That I had to molt and break
While a new avatar I take.
I am a learner
Every passing second

And the urge to change the heart
Is clearer.
You are kindness and love,
I realize my craving,
My need, my necessity
To constantly be in Your grace
To consistently get closer
And someday be one.

LEAVING

The little voice says: "don't go"
It's hard to leave the shore.
Ships sail into the unknown
Before you know it, you're gone.

Go in the spirit, trusting.
It's going to a destiny
That you were born with.
Make faith your identity.

Go with peace, look ahead.
Cherish the backward glance
To the book not read
Or the untaken chance.

If you try to look back.
You don't remember the last year.
The last kiss. The last goodbye.
So just let go without the fear.

THE REALITY OF GOD

The abiding reality of God
Are my moments in time
His will shape my moments
I believe they're mine.

The call of God is like the call of the sea
You cannot hear or envision it
But you know that when you are ready
You respond to His spirit.

Try to not dig and toil into
What His purpose is for you.
There is wisdom that shapes our end
And divinity that prompts your mend

HE WORKETH

Roll it over, pass the buck
He works on it in his time
Worry not. It's going to be fine
Hand it over, you're in luck!

He takes it, but you must trust
In your accepting faith and lest
You think that life's unjust
Remember that it's your mistrust

Roll out, roll out upon Him
Your cares, no matter how grim
Your faith tested to the very brim
He answers the prayer and the hymn.

HOPE

There's a hole in my soul
Where hope would be.
It fell out the bottom
And I felt free.

There's so much hope
In depending on Him

He is the promise
He's paid for the sin.

The hope is not bound now
To my mortal core
It is a promise of treasures
For evermore.

MYSTERY

SACRED IDLENESS

Got greeted by the fog at dawn
It swept away into a cloud.
Every hidden mystery was torn
Revealing the birds' clear sound.

Listen, hear and see the ray of sun
As it hits the celestial road
Reaching the earth to make the day
And gently ease my load.

The droplets, the fog, the ray rolls on
My very being in glory.
Precious is each part of every day.
I'm here and telling my story..

PIE IN THE SKY

Faithful in its rising
And waning in its precision
Tho' always a step behind
That orb that blinds.
But if ever you turn out to be a disciple
Of Diana or Artemus or of the Creator
Or a lunatic you be,
You know it had you at the first hello!
And at the Crescent or the half
Or even at the cheese-in-the-sky phase
Of which is decided the months and times
And always the tides.
Ever seen it behind the trees or clouds
Peeping like a shy maid
Or in its full glory
On a clear stage?
Lunatic I might be
But for me to the moon and back
Is the measure of my heartbeat
Because that is my beloved pie in the sky.
The calm, the cool, the ice to my fire.
The peace in my soul.

JOURNALING

I cannot journal unless my pencil is sharp.
Does that mean something?
Or does being in Spirit make it so....
Everything takes on a new meaning now
Everything has a glow.

I carry with me the murmurs of raw voices
The whispers of consolation
Knowing in my heart
God moves through the ages
Goodness is timeless and endless.

There for the taking and the taker
It needs to be repeated
And repeated and repeated
Ever circling around in ripples

Verses written at a workshop on journaling during an online conference on mysticism

MY FATE WITH CANCER

Buried in my genetic past
All these budding lymphs,
Old wine in new bottles?
Left porta hepatic, right encasing renal artery
Just onslaught battery!
Don't know where you're going cancer.
Right out the door, I hope.
Don't mess with danger.
I'm not one to mope.
I don't know you, but old friend
Maybe you're the foe
With this lymphatic trend
I want nothing to do with you anymore.
So, hey you, cancer.
You come from ago.
Rad51 is the gene
That makes you go.
Buried in my genetic past
You mutated in my core.
My double helix let me down
Nothing I can do anymore.
But wait you're history now
At least to me.
Spare my progeny.
In peace let them be.

FEAR DISPELS, DOUBTS SCATTER

Grey, foggy clouds obscuring the heavens
The heights unimaginable where He dwells.
The place in your heart he inhabits within
Where the grey clouds now swell.

But you can see a thousand clear stars
They glimmer, their glow even shatters
The fog around your heart,
Fear dispels, doubts scatter
As uncertainty crashes
Into a thousand shards

The stars are above space and matter
Clear as the heavens in your heart;
In this room where you lie in bed
And gaze wide-eyed at the Creator

LIFE'S CHALLENGE

THE FIRMAMENT

I'm counting the stars on your ceiling.
That you installed with so much care.
Bright, brilliant and dozens of them there.
Enduring and permanent, unpeeling.

Hidden in glory when it's bright
I wait in patience for the dark.
When they appear in a flash of light
I sense the Creator's spark.

God in the beginning of time.....
Wrote your destiny as your stars were hung.
Each one a blessing, each one your cross
Revealed as a step on a ladder's rung.

Maybe this is what is Life.
You must climb to reach for your stars
Not when you're bathed in sunlight
But in the dark moments of the night.

Hang in there with both hands.
Keep climbing. He's got you.
In the starlight glow of your blessings
He hung them there just for you!

THE CRUCIBLE

Live each day, doing what must be done.
Be it normal, or routine or a trivial one.
Give of yourself to someone or to a task,
Of yourself, expect much, but little ask.

Change becomes reality,
When you accept it and see the sense
In what's on the other side you can't see.
It's greener when you get off the fence.

I have a program. I have a plan.
The hour glass keeps running out of sand.
I may not follow my agenda exactly,
But about that I won't feel too badly.

He who permits the suffering
Is with us in it.
We see Him while the trail is passing.
He never leaves the crucible.

THE GIFT

God gifted me myself,
Pure in my mother's womb.
Did I gift to God what I became
Stuck in a spiritual tomb?

I have to give Him back
What I can become
A giving me, a kinder me
and then some.

The spiritual law that I want to choose
of believing, abiding and holding steady.
Is a rock of faith I cannot lose.
He strengthens and settles me daily.

God, give me the courage to ask You.
Grant me the quiet to hear You.
Give me the grace to listen to You.
The wisdom to know when to beg of You.

But always Lord, Your Will.

With apologies to Reinhold Niebuhr's Serenity Prayer

TOMORROW TODAY

History wasn't yesterday
Or the past in a flash;
It is present in today
Fleeting in a mad dash.

The events of the hours
The fall of the dice
The building of the towers
Can crumble in a thrice.

The wall, the monuments
Built in hundred years or ten
Each brick, stone and tent
Dug up today was foundation then.

Your today will write tomorrow
Each minute constructed well.
Be it joys, kindness or sorrow
The remains a story will tell.

THE SONG
OF THE LION

It matters not what comes your way
A meek lamb or a lion wild
On your path you have to stay
Be triumphant or reconciled.

The Lion was the option for David
Stay a herder or be a king
Grow into the man or stay a kid
Nothing lost or gained a herder being.

But kings can read and write and sing
Win battles and make the plan
Use his fortunes and more for doing
Great things for God and man.

Your lion can come to you whenever
Wherever He sends it to you
Use the battle through pain, however
To praise the Lord, give Him the due.

LET THE
KINDNESS OUT

The window opens but a slit
To let the kindness out
And glimpses an old but fresh soul
Before it shuts out in the cold.

Lonely is the soul unless you
Open the window, the peek into heaven
You can be bathed in the light,
If that open window is within sight.

Give me a clean heart
And renew my spirit
Live and let live, let go, let go
Till the cobwebs are no more.

Start anew with a child-like mind
A heart so clean is hard to find
But a deed a day, a good thought
And half your battle is fought.

JOURNEYS & DESTINATIONS

The engine of the mind
Disconnects from the bogies of the body.
One stands still by the tracks
Plumes of smoke fly by from the other.
Stay still. Move.
Sometimes it appeals.
This sense of disconnection
The needle out of the groove.
But the joys of journeys in harmony
Must cast a shadow over destination
The cares, the burdens, the frustration.
This is life. We're all not Desert Monks

TIME ZONES

Where you are, the birds sing
The koyal calls and peacocks dance.
In the lane, the children call
And life begins again.
I lay my weary head
On my way to dreams
To rest, to oblivion.
Nestling in the cocoon of night
Our dreams never meeting

BASK IN THE SUN

Ditch the projects
And enjoy the day
Zooms, studies, texts...
Leave them by the way.

Doing nothing, basking
In the sun, under the sky
In the garden pottering
While hearing birds fly.

Flowers in a line
Watching the cloud
Not wasting time
Proclaiming that loud

Every unaccounted minute
As it ticks away
The day has lots in it
You have to unlock the way.

GET OFF
THE WHEEL

You can be a Sufi dancer
And be still.
You can dance in the storm
And be calm if you will.

Swirling body, whirling mind
But peace within, stillness inside
The momentum carries you away
Into perpetual motioning sway

Like the pendulum to and fro
The tasks increase and grow.
Stop, stop get off the wheel
Sit by the gentle flow and feel.

The rhythm of your heart and soul
Slowing down to clinch your goal.
Be that your next task, another day
Something urgent, or just fun and play

A half-read book, an incomplete prayer
A pending poem or just...sit and stare.

TURMOIL

Much unspoken, much unsaid
Emotions largely unexpressed
It erupts in heaving turmoil
Was it dormant? Was it never?

Running in circles, much undone.
Whirling agenda on the run
Time fleeting, yet not really.
Time in the glass? The grains all gone?

Much to accomplish, self-expectations
Unfinished business, yet never started.
The plans, the lists, the drawing board.
Was it ever purposed? Was it ever?

Choices chosen, choices regretted.
Then back to form, forgiveness pleaded
Grace and forgiveness erupt within
Did the tide turn? Did life change?
Peace!

THE LIGHT OF THE WORLD

You make the crib.
Angels , donkey, stars and sheep
And when it's time
You place Him in....
The light of the world
His little hands reaching out
WHAT DOES HE SEE?
You, only you
As you make Him your centre,
Your all.

Years go by, life gets busy.
You're rushing
To tick off that long Xmas list.
But occasionally catch a glimpse...
He's still in that crib
at Macy's or Hamleys.
He's caught your eye
WHAT DOES HE SEE?
A fine young lady or man
Rushing thru life.
Where and who is the
Light of your world?
He waits till once again
You might make Him your centre.

More hectic years tick by..
You're back making a crib
For little ones who excitedly
Place Him back
In shiny wonder.
WHAT DOES HE SEE?
Ahhh yes...
He's still the light of your nest
Your home.

Some are privileged and blessed
To return to the light.
Some never left sight
Of the Logos
Which was with God
And which became God
on Earth.
WHAT DOES HE SEE?
A faithful beloved
Who has acknowledged that light
As a guide, a lamp for your feet.
Shine on so you reflect
His spirit, His light !

LADDERING AND SNAKING

Always wanting to be up in the spirit,
Forcing, cajoling, begging.
Sometimes, a good, solid kick does it.
Don't throw the dice.
Up, up the ladder
The journey up is euphonious,
Worthy, spirit-lifting, glorious
No. There are no snakes on this board.

THE FLIGHT OF THE KITE

Sometimes the way to calm down
Is to be a kite
Fly high
And be out of sight.
Find air and float
In super oxygen
Till you can, till you can
Come back.
And be yourself
Whatever that is for the moment
Be there for them
Whoever they are at this moment
And just be content. Just Be.

Book Two

REFLECTIONS

An introspection of thoughts and
scriptures
that have inspired and influenced my life

My Cancer Recovery Mission Statement

On 08 July 2018, I took that intuitive decision when told of my cancer diagnosis. The decision was to grab His hand in faith as I move into this cataclysmic, scary unknown awaiting me.

Surprisingly, I did not pray for my own healing. I don't remember saying: "Lord, heal me of this cancer."

All I remember chanting over and over again, at every stage of diagnosis, treatment, surgery and now at recovery is this: "Lord, be with me and give me your strength and give me the gift of faith in Your will. I trust and surrender."

Today, I am healed in my soul. My Gethsamane.

SCRIPTURE

So, we see they were not able to enter due to their disbelief.
Hebrews 3:18-19

Coming out of Egypt for the Israelites was a journey I relate to. Just as coming out of our weaknesses is a means to Hope. The long journey I have begun is not only to cope with my cancer, but, instead, to come into the fullness of Christ, where I may have His grace, sufficient to me, and make His spirit work in me so as to become a blessing to others. I have to remember His grace. Always being with me, His spirit works and is manifested in my life.

 Every phone call I receive, every text message, every moment someone reaches out to help, every second that Robin attends to me, I see His grace reaching out to me.

 No negatives. No looking at this illness as a deterrent. Maybe, I am blessed to be able to "rest in His

sufficiency."

      Help me Lord to be a blessing to others. "His power is made perfect in all our weaknesses." You know mine, Lord: physical and mental weaknesses bring my spirit down.

Come unto me, all ye that labour and are heavy laden, and I will give you rest. Take my yoke upon you, and learn of me; for I am meek and lowly in heart and ye shall find rest unto your souls. For my yoke is easy, and my burden is light. (Matthew 11:28-30)

Yes, it is because You carry the yoke, Lord, that my burden is light. I mean to remember that when people and things strike from all sides and I get so involved with trying to cope on my own, that the yoke shifts from my side to yours.

      I am trying to absorb the blows coming into my life. So, I focus on Christ holding my hand. I can do this by absorbing Him into my being. Or else just a rude word, ugly accusations and

feelings of defenselessness and utter unworthiness can overwhelm me. Life would be reduced to such a fruitless, useless existence.

Lord I start from the bottom up. But thank you for the shake-up, which helps me remember that you are still here with me. I will follow you with my broken spirit.

My cancer has made me focus on Jesus all the more! I am with Him ...a hanger on a groupie. I am trying to bring about a change in me. But I know how impossible this is without prayer. Prayer is the power and silence, the source of strength no matter how impossible and hopeless it seems. Grace in perseverance.

Then Moses said to the Israelites, "See, the LORD has chosen Bezalel, son of Uri, the son of Hur, of the tribe of Judah, and he has filled him with the Spirit of God, with wisdom, with understanding, with knowledge and with all kinds of skills."
(Exodus 35:30-31)

Bezalel worked with gold, silver, bronze, wood and metal to craft the Arc of he Covenant. This is my kind of God-bestowed skills. To work with our hands is not something we normally associate with the need to be filled with the Holy Spirit.

But I like to think that there is an eternal dimension of a divine agenda behind the daily grind. I know the Mass experience is the source of the inspiration for bringing into my daily life a fire and zeal to cook that roast beef or crochet that angel or install that overhead light.

I love the sense of being equipped to take the Spirit and bring God back with us into our homes and community and spread it among our far-flung families.

I would love to share more images of what I have been inspired to do with my hands which is a conduit for God's glory, just as Bezalel worked on building the first Holy Covenant to house the Ten Commandments. It is about looking beyond the mundane to the magnificent

and seeing a much bigger picture of why God has placed us where we are to display His glory.

Mocking Words

Lord, I'm trying to be at your side... though I know you have never moved away from mine. Tonight, I dwelt on Jeremiah 23:9 "My heart is broken within me – all my bones tremble." People say things and you begin to doubt your worth. Nathaniel's mocking words: "Can any good come out of Nazareth," (John 1: 46) fell on deaf ears: Jesus came out of that land. Be with me Lord.

"You, yourselves give them something to eat." (Mark 6: 37)

I cook and cook again. I plan food. I read, watch and dream food. I love the history of food. It soothes me and is my past-time and hobby. How much of this interest and love do I share with the world that needs food? None. So, here's

something to add to my TO-DO-FOR-OTHERS list. Cook for the kitchens of the needy or donate to food banks.

He would go away to lonely places, where he prayed. (Luke 5:16)

Daily prayer needs a lonely place. Most often I find that lonely place in my heart. I like to lick my wounds that I, myself, inflict there on account of my overbearing speech, although not meaning to hurt people and especially the one I love. In the process I hurt myself. My resolution: Speak Gently, especially when irate!

The spirit of the Lord is upon me, because He has chosen me to bring good news to the poor! (Luke 4:17-18)

I had a chemo session today: calm, uneventful but successful. I was watching a documentary (at the same time) on Italian Chef Massimo who started a soup kitchen in Italy where chefs from the

world come in to cook their gourmet meals for refugees. Caritas is a partner. Evangelism is one beggar telling another beggar where to find bread. My evangelism of bread is unfolding slowly. Choose me Lord!

"He must increase, but I must decrease." (John: 3:30)

How I wish I could deflect, in this illness phase, the focus on me, so I can be a witness to these abundant gifts of faith and belief. What can I do to point everyone in His direction? His is the face people should see me reflecting.

"This is my own dear Son, with whom I am pleased." (Matt. 3:16-17)

The Son of God died. It is, by all means, to be believed because it is absurd. And He was buried and rose again. It is certain because it is impossible! Tertullion (160 AD-240 AD)

I struggle with the magnanimity of this reality, but God's love for humans is seen so clearly. His hope for humanity evidenced through the prophets. I know that His is the Face that hovered over the face of the earth and the water and everything was created!

"The Sabbath was made for the good of man. Man was not made for the Sabbath." (Mark 2: 27)

How we lose perspective of another human being! We program the way someone should behave in relation to us. Doesn't work that way! Lord, open my eyes fully and my heart wholly and my ears soundly to listen to another, to let them be who they are.

"Even so faith, if it hath not works, is dead, being alone." (James 2:17)

Today, we missed a collision on Main

Street. Crazy driver broke the red light! Faith requires action, and not just belief. We express faith. I do, to myself. Witnessing not much. But Robin decided to share Christ with friends on Facebook to relate his faith in the Lord with reference to yesterday's near-miss collision with that crazy driver. I trust God whole-heartedly to part the seas. Give me the courage and this is the time I need the faith to turn belief into action.

"Happy are those who know they are spiritually poor; the kingdom of God belongs to them." (Matt 5:3)

To be poor in spirit is to realize that we cannot go through life alone. There will be times when even our friends cannot help us, much as they want to and we want them to. Concern, fatigue, life, space, time are human aspects. Jesus said: **"I am the vine, you are the branches. You can do nothing without me."** (John 15:5)

The Beatitude that stands out for me is this: **"Blessed are the poor in spirit, for they shall see God."**

It refers to spiritual poverty: a state of being when you realize that not everything is in your hands and you depend on God who controls all. The grace you receive, acknowledging and being spiritually poor is a blessing.

Christmas is Incarnation

It's God's actual entry into history. It was the flash point in time when He embraced the world. His reaching out to Adam was the promise. Christmas was the promise fulfilled.

Christmas is Incarnation and also the Resurrection. God stepping out of the cloud and arriving here, but not departing. He came with nothing on that silent night and has not left. An arrival without a departure.

He lives here, till we are able to hear him with the ears of our heart and

the eyes of our heart. Until then we will not grasp the proof of His existence.

He will bring down your high, fortified walls and lay them low. He will bring them down to the ground, to the very dust. (Isaiah 25: 12)

The weak links in my fort are my eyes and ears. The heart and mind, even though they respond to these stimuli, are in my Lord's hands. But one in the first line of defense are those "occuli" which absorb the sights of the world, the things my eyes read and see and absorb.

Help me see with your eyes, Lord. The next are my ears – those "aurem" that are taking in sound waves.

Help me hear the world's cries and anger and joy through my "aurem cordi" Lord.

FAITH

"Lord, if it's you," Peter replied, **"tell me to come to you on the water."**
"Come," he said. (Matt: 14: 28-31)

This is my favourite Bible account. I took that step out of the boat on the 8th of July 2018 in that emergency room of the hospital, when the doctor came in saying: "Sorry, I have no good news for you. You have cancer."

I wasn't brave. But I displayed bravado. I wasn't shocked. I was numb. I wasn't worried about myself. I was worrying about everyone.

When did I step out on the water? Later.... when the Lord had said: "Come." Am I still on the water? I think I am... but sometimes it feels like a somewhat stormy sea.

"Courage! It is I. Don't be afraid."
(Mark 6:50-51)

Then He got into the boat with them. (A different version from Matthew's gospel) Jesus asks Peter to step out towards him and he does!
    Lord, I am still out, standing on water with you, with the faith you're gifting me. But if you want to lead me back to the boat and get in with me, I will surrender to you. It has taken a lot of myself, but I can gladly stand as well. You're with me!!!

"The One who calls you is faithful and He will do it." (Thessalonians 5:24)

When Moses reached the promised land, he sent out twelve spies: two of them Joshua and Caleb, saw strong, fortified Canaan through the eyes of faith, but ten voted for not entering the promised land. They did not combine what they knew about God with their faith in Him. And

they wandered for thirty eight more years!

Lord, as you walk with me and I see those single set of footprints amid my tribulation, I know it is then when you, unfailingly, carry me.

"A gracious woman gains respect."
(Proverbs 11:16)

Grace, gentleness and empathy are virtues I used to have, I think. What happened? I feel like I'm a metal plate forged and beaten in a Smitty's fire...and have not come out truly refined, neither well-shaped nor nice to touch.
What happened?

How might I open my heart more fully to the action of the Spirit in my life? I marvel at the twelve apostles. I admire the faith of the thousands who heard Jesus and were rewarded by the Great overwhelming, outpouring gift of faith.

Maybe I always took this gift for granted. Maybe I need to go back to join the crowds on the Galilee shore or the

House He entered in Nazareth..

Fear Not!
"Perfect love casts out all fear."
(John 4:18)

I had to dig deep into my heart and drag out all my faith and courage and step fearlessly into the Covid Testing Centre. (The Lord is my rock, my fortress and my deliverer – Psalm 18:2)

    God actually commands us not to fear or worry. But we're human and submit to fear. God knows that the outside forces used fear to deplete our hope and weaken our faith. The words "fear not" are used at least 365 times in the Bible.

Be Still and Know That I am God.
(Psalm 46:10)

All I could hear was the rustling of the leaves and distant car sounds. I looked up and two clouds were ambling away with purpose. Going east to a destination.

I watched. I tried to lighten myself to reach into some inner space within and asked the Lord to hold my hand and reach in with me. What did we lay hands on?

He gave me fear. Very deep, inner fear that I didn't even know existed. In all my troubling times of pain. It must have been there and I had to overcome it with belief and prayer, for courage, trust and faith, He gave me in abundance.

But I now realized He had given me all these gifts, those graces to counter that which was lurking there: Fear.

"Fear Not," He said. "I have redeemed you. I have summoned you by name. You are mine." Isaiah 43:1

So, I know that though inner fear might rise again with every occasion, mine are not the hands that will pluck it out from the dark insides; mine will not be the hands sending it away, resolutely away like the clouds.

Be a river, not a reservoir of God's mercy. No one lives to himself and no one dies to himself. (Romans 14:7)

People preoccupied with their own holiness and spirituality are really reservoirs till they make themselves rivers that flow. Genuinely holy people are preoccupied with God and it is the faithfulness of our obedience to Him and our dependence on Him that is a measure of our lives.

"Daughter your faith has made you well. Go in peace and be healed."
(Mark 5: 34)

Persistence in faith is not that which allows the body and spirit to heal. It is the work of God and not earned by human effort. To be bold in what we believe is to not be deterred by circumstance or discouraged by others. It's God's grace which is granted to you.

"All things are possible to him that

believes." (Mark 9:23). Jarius' daughter was brought back to life. **"I say to you little girl, arise."** (Mark 5:21-43)

"Come," he said. Then Peter got out of the boat, walked on the water and came toward Jesus. (Matt 14: 29)

We have an idea that God is leading us to a particular end, a goal. And I've always thought that one day God will show me His purpose. A clear goal and then I can fulfill it.

But, I think, this very journey is the purpose. So, I depend on Him and His power now. God's goal or end is to enable me to see that He can walk on the chaos of my life right now and make each moment precious.

.

SELF INTROSPECTION

Let Old Acquaintance Be Forgot

The sun set somewhere in the clouds last night. It will rise without the stale air surrounding it. Old stale deeds, opportunities missed, baggage....In the light of a New Year, shed away. As a big cleansing fire is lit. Another gift of a beautiful year gone. I have hopefully used it well. I was with all my three children, their spouses and my grandkids at the stroke of midnight. But I look at Robin and see weary eyes and the toll life has taken on him. I hope he encounters all the joy of our life together, as much as I do.

    I am trying to offload some resentments. Trying to remind myself that I am just here to help people move along. And I keep that thought in mind when resentment lingers and crumbles before it blooms. Important events in someone else's life don't have to always include me.

Who am I really, in the big scheme of things. Move on in thoughts, words, reactions, deeds. And forgive, forget, love.

Thank you for loving me.

God is unconditionally forgiving, when I do wrong. He wants for me to realize it and come back to Him with my contrition. Sometimes I need His help to open my eyes to my faults.
    Dear Robin, so concerned with utter love, feels wounded and hurt to see me unwell. I want to give him myself, healthy and whole. Dear family: a vessel of unconditional love...now beginning to see a mom with clay feet. Dear friends....they accept.

I am weak

I am a fort. Strong but still vulnerable. But in Isaiah 25:12, we read: "The unassailable fortifications of your walls He will bring down low and cast to the

ground, even to the dust."

The weak links in my fort are my eyes and ears. The heart and mind, even though they respond to these stimuli are in my Lord's hands. But the ones in the first line of defense are those eyes which absorb the sights and the world, the things my eyes read and see. Help me see with your eyes, Lord.

The next my ears. Help me hear the world's cries and pleas and anger and joy through my "eyes and ears" Lord.

MYSTERY

In the Silence

"There is silence into which the world cannot intrude. You carry an ancient peace in your heart that you have not lost." A Course in Miracles by Helen Schucman.

But why am I doing this "silence exercise"? Most often I hear the quiet voice in my non-still moments. The

silence exercise makes me conscious of my breath.

"God is the breath inside the breath." said the poet Kabir. I will find him there.

Being Still

Listening to my breathing. Again, what is the purpose of being still? Is it to finally enter into the Lord's presence in a different way? I feel I am in His presence at odd moments in the day. I know the Lord is with me.

I woke up to a stillness and continued to be in the stillness. Silence. Silence all around. My body stilled and mind stilled. Words came to me that I can't remember clearly this morning on waking up.

But a lingering memory of feet? May be two sets of feet? I can remember the feeling of wanting to take these steps to leave this place? To walk with these other feet besides mine. I can't remember the picture at all, but the feeling of security is what I recall.

Dream

I'm in the dark, stone-Monte-Cristo-type cave. And the torch runs out of battery. It gets pitch dark. And I am terrified and panic-stricken. I make my way to the solid wooden door and shout: "Help me. Help me." I banged on the deaf door. Then I gather my courage and say: "It's okay. Jesus is here." I try to make my way around in the stark darkness muttering: "I'll get used to it. I just have to let my eyes adjust and my vision will be fortified." I woke up. I tried to go back to sleep and just as it was overtaking me, I see the same scenario. Only this time the door is wide open and someone's saying: "Go...go."
I hesitate, unbelieving. Then the voice returns – this time somewhat frantic and impatient and loud. "Just go, go, go."

"Try to be the rainbow in someone else's cloud." Maya Angelou

Clouds are the reflections of the sorrows and suffering in our own lives or in the lives of others. It is by those very clouds that the spirit of God is urging us to walk by faith. God cannot come near without clouds. It's not as if God is teaching us a lesson. Perhaps, he wants us to unlearn something. It will get darker if there is anyone else in it, save Jesus. He does not come on a clear day.

Created in His image and likeness

We are created in God's image and likeness. God's goal in creating us is for us to become like Him in holiness and love. "You shall be holy, for I, the Lord your God am holy." (Leviticus 19:2) We cannot do this without preparation. Prepare our bodies, our minds and our spirit in little steps, in stages, in prayer, in seeing God's image and likeness in other humans and in Creation.

TRIAL AND SUFFERING

My Thin Place

It's an ancient concept: Thin places are those rare locales where the distance between Heaven and Earth converge. A good example would be the biblical connection to locations like Mt. Sinai or Horeb.

But thin spaces happen in everyday life in the midst of trouble, painful moments; being intimate with fear. It is a moment of clarity for me, lying on a hospital bed on a summer's day in July 2018.

I had to draw on some inner core faith in the Creator who has charge of me. That's when I made a connection. It was as if a narrow path was seen in a previously rock strewn area. I felt like all I had to do was put my foot on that path. It seemed treacherous and I didn't know if it would continue.

All in a flash! In maybe 10

seconds – all of this was reality. Then when I looked at the devastated-stricken faces of family and friends around me... I knew I had to take that step of faith.

The Chosen

He has chosen me. It's not that I have chosen Him. So, I am sitting alone in the chemo room Pod-2 getting a dose of Caelyx and Carboplatin. Alone with my Lord and not connected to the world. (Those memories of Covid-19 protocol come back to me). Alone, but never afraid. The blessings of the Lord come with no sorrow in tow.

Trust and Submission

Another futile blood test: Those neutrophils are way under the normal count. I just have to accept these road bumps. They get me where I am going in the Lord's time...not mine. I have stopped setting the clock to my timeline. It ticks at His pace. But I wonder in the

meantime: What is the meaning, the plan or is there none. Just be still? In Him? Just look at His face and worship!!

My Gethsemane

Now, I feel Gethsemane. It has just skimmed off my soul. Now I know the fear of not knowing. So I ask: Was standing on the water with you all these years, just a rehearsal for plunging into the deep? A totally scary deep dive.

    I could cope with the surface, the storms, the waves, the plunges, the howling wind. You are always there. But now you want me to dive deep? I have always loved the ocean. Never truly gave thought to its unknown, dark depths. But now to hold my breath and dive in with you?

    Ah! Is this, what going down below to "helplessness" and self-doubt and a slightly false-bravado is all about? Now I have to shed my armor, my shell and like the conch leave it on the shore, amongst the softly lapping gently ebbing tides of

time. Now is the time to capitalize the mere words ACCEPTANCE AND TRUST. Underneath each deeper wave is your invitation to see with new eyes. A different view of life to seek you anew and know that you are my God. And like the starfish, go back to the salty, stinging ocean to survive.

Being in darkness

It's one week into that scan that made me physically ill and put me in a dark spot spiritually and mentally. No rays of sun outside nor inside me. Where did my light go? But not a doubt that it would rise again. Inside my heart. I had to just keep praying.

It's not the physical lows that really count: scans, chemo, diarrhea bouts, insomnias...bring them all on! But it's the darkness of the soul that brings me closer to the Creator. Are you in the dark just now in your circumstances, or in your life with God? Then stay still. Darkness is the time to listen. I'm learning to deal with the shadows. How slow I have been to

understand that like Christ, humility is the gift of the biggest pain.

INTERFACE WITH GOD

Thank you, Father

The earth rotated again and I with it. I touched the earth and moved and laughed and saw the sky. Even as my spirit flew, You kept me tethered down here below where I perhaps need to be so as to grow where you plant me. Keep the joy in me alive. Please let me create my happy sphere to radiate your gift of a spirit which is in need of renewal every time!

A Prayer

O Lord, help me to be more positive about everything. I have a positive outlook. I know that to be one of the gifts that you bestowed on me. You have also generously thrown another in the gift basket: my fighting spirit! I ask very humbly that you

give me a booster dose of both. I'll take it from there with You by my side. If you can fill up my slowly depleting, half-empty glass back to being half full again... for this I pray.

I am the Lord's YoYo

He is my Maker and my Breaker. I am clay in His hands. I think He needs to break me when He thinks He is not happy with the present version of me. When He thinks He can make a better me. Whatever version of perfection He sees me as. Someday, I will be His idea of a perfect me...And he will keep me close to Him, forever.

The Dislodged Log

Dear Lord: Let me be that branch of a tree. A stout log that when dislodged during a storm in turbulent surroundings and emotional upheavals, just bobs, staying afloat, with your mercy and love. It just bobs on the mad crazy waves, gets bashed on the jutting river boulders, gets

snagged by the gnarled roots and tangled reeds. It just bobs along, staying calm and afloat in your promise and love. It gets lighter and detached from the restless river surrounding it. Just **bobbing…with faith, in the path …to you.**

I am like broken pottery.
(Psalm 31:12)

I have become like broken pottery. Yet, Lord, you are the potter and I am the clay. You can remold and make me anew. Today, I was singing "Into your hands I commend my Spirit." Deliver me Lord. My faithful God. Keep me free from the traps set for me: my overconfidence, too much cockiness, false pride in my good health and the sense that I have to be strong for everyone else. Dear God, I am your humble child and I come to you for refuge. Be my rock.

Forgiveness Ends Hate

The inner turmoil and past experiences are hard, heavy loads to carry. How much gunk and garbage we carry through the years. We burden ourselves and can't let go. Why is it that we remember past hurts and negative feelings with a vengeance. It's just being human. How hard it is to be like Christ, forgiving to the bitter end.

"Forget the former things. Do not dwell in the past. See I am making a way in the wilderness and streams in the Wasteland." (Isaiah 43:19)

May Day

Early morning call and airport drop for Aaron, my son. So much sadness to part from him and from the girls: Golda and Esther. But so much thankfulness for the children in our lives. They couldn't have been bigger blessings for us. They have been our rock. My rocks. Like the display ones I have on my kitchen shelf.

The Lord sends his rocks spreading their ripples in the waters of my life.

Contentment

Contentment is a very big reward for a little thing: No need. No want. A garden to potter around, a sewing project, cooking a good meal, hot coffee, a long walk in the sun, zooming with family...is all it takes. Gone are the stresses, worries, sleepless nights. Gone with the years! God grant me serenity.

Do what you can with what you have.

What am I meant to do with my life? Surely, there must be a higher purpose. Being of help to someone? Joining an organized volunteer group? I am doing whatever I can with whatever I have. I'm cooking, cleaning, sewing, reading, trying new skills, gardening, tidying up, doing laundry and zooming. I try to do these things with care, wisdom and grace.
    "Therefore do not worry about tomorrow, for tomorrow will worry about its own things. Sufficient for the day is its

own troubles." (Matt 6:34)

Shove it in and let it go!

It's been a journey! Sixty-six years and going! It's 1919. My life's been a fortunate one. I've always been given three square meals, a roof over my head and much more: friends, loving family, wonderful children with wonderful spouses, great super-grand children and a most loving, caring husband.

And still, there's always this room of things I've locked away. Probably so full that it has jammed the door and I can't open it anymore, which might be a good thing: A room of would-haves, could-haves, what ifs, and should-haves, I-could-have done-more, things-never-attempted. This room, I dedicate to my loving Lord, my eternal Father, who knows what's best for me and gave me this bin to shove things in! "Shove it in and let it go," He says. Someday the garbage man will take it all out of your life.

Faith Is Lifelong

Robin and I joined the Walk-for-Cancer fund raiser and reminisced about the events since my cancer diagnosis! Thank you, my Lord. You've helped me walk the walk with faith and talk the talk about you. Not enough though. Faith is a lifelong journey. You fall and you get up.

Restore My Spirit, Lord.

I picked up a verse from the Bread of Life card pack today and here's what I got: "I give you strength, I bring you help. I uphold you with my victorious hand." (Isaiah 41:10)

Lord, every good deed and every ounce of good in me comes from You. I just took my various good virtues for granted little realizing that they are gifts from You: my humor, my good will and my usually generous nature. I ask and beg of You now for those to be restored and my Spirit to be renewed.

Listening to God

How do I obey God when I don't hear a command. How do I discern when the Lord speaks? How and where do I seek His message. I need to wait in order to listen to His voice: Where? How? When? (Isaiah 6:8) "I heard the voice of God saying whom shall I send. And who will go for us?" And I said, "Here am I, Send me." Lord may I see and hear with the eyes and ears of my heart.

O Wondrous Creator

O creator who hung the firmament over the waters, defying our earthly laws as we try to understand what is up in the spire from the basement below, grant humanity your indulgence.

    O divine artist, who bestowed on the weavers of nature the ability to design every delicate, beautiful web glistening in dew drops— an instinctive gift of subsistence—grant humanity the faith of the lilies of the field.

    O lord of nature, mother of a

nurturing earth and of the infinite universe, give us the wisdom to know that we are in the birthing stage of understanding and grant humanity the patience and the wisdom, to treasure and nourish without destroying that which you have provided here, before we venture there, into your ancient, unfathomable vastness.

ACKNOWLEDGEMENTS

As far as I can remember, I was always passionate about poetry—the sound and the rhythm of its language and the metaphor in which it expresses itself. So, although I turned to science for a career, I never abandoned poetry—the reading or writing of it.

    I write short poems because most likely I'm impulsively obeying the Muse around my pots and pans or sometimes at dead of night or in the wee hours of the morning while scrambling for a piece of paper and a pencil or frantically seeking a journal among the many strewn all over the house. I chase the will-o-the-wisp to turn a thought into a rhyme. So most often I rummage through backs of store receipts, or kitchen towels, or even toilet paper—there's always a pencil stuck in the tooth brush mug—to find my poems.

    But these many years, I have been inspired by a host of poets, theologians, mystics, and spiritualists. My poems and

reflections have been inspired, in part, by their wisdom. Among them are people such as Richard Rohr, Bishop Robert Baron, Rumi, Omar Khayam, Tertullian (160 AD-240 AD) Kabir Das, Mother Teresa, Julian of Norwich, Saint Francis of Assi, Maya Angelou, and many other special people including Fr. Owen Connolly, Dinah Simmons, and others who have been an inspiration to me. I acknowledge all of them with gratitude.

I have been inspired, too, with books such as L. B. Cowman's *Streams in the Desert*, Pope Benedict XVI's *Jesus of Nazareth* (Vols. I an II), and *A Course in Miracles* by Helen Schucman. But above everything else, Holy Scripture has been my guiding light and has influenced my work.

In a special way, I acknowledge the support from Dr. Sebastian Mahfood, OP, of En Route Books and Media, who has made the publishing of this book possible. Thank you, Dr. Mahfood.

But these poems and reflections

would be in their various scattered nests, lying dormant, if it wasn't for my husband, Robin, who diligently, patiently and very professionally rescued them so they could bring life to these pages. This really is for you, Rob. Thank you love!

    Lastly, but not the least, I am grateful to my family, who have been my closest confidants and my everything. Thank you, my darlings.

Teresa Arthur, abandoned a career as a doctor, not wanting to risk a burning flame of love in Bombay melt away while studying medicine in a city 600 kms away. A science graduate at the time, she, instead, taught science and chemistry, first in India, later in the United Arab Emirates and lastly in Canada.

An ardent reader of history and fiction and a culinary wizard in multi-ethnic cuisine, she had never made known her secret passion for poetry, her soul's freedom and her heart's mouthpiece. So, in time, verses poured out on the pages of her journals every time beauty and truth would awaken her.

But when in July 2018 a cancer diagnosis came down on her like a ton of bricks, she sharpened her pencils, and her verses shifted focus to thoughts on faith, the mystical, creation, human suffering, and, above all, the gospels of Jesus Christ.

She and her husband Robin live in Halifax. They have three children and seven grandchildren.

Take off your shoes;
you are standing on holy ground.

Isn't that the feeling we get when we are privileged to be let into someone's most private thoughts, when they open their hearts and souls to us? That's what Teresa Arthur has done in *Talking to Myself.* She shares her inner life, the things she says to herself and the things she says to God: ordinary, everyday things—but touched by the shadow of cancer and kindled by the presence of God.

Teresa's poems focus on simple things: seeing one year out and a new one in; fixating at the moon and the stars, morning fog, the sound of birds. Cancer is not the protagonist in the narrative, although its shadow lingers. There's shock and fear; pain and sickness; there's worry for herself and for her loved ones and the prayer that her children may never have to go through this. But above that, there's faith, a brave, beautiful faith present in everything: her sharpened pencil, the garden she tends, the food she cooks... every little part of her story, is part of a bigger story, God's story.

Teresa writes with so much honesty and courage, so much humility and love, inviting us into her musings, into her life. When someone opens up to you, shares their vulnerability, it's an invitation, an opportunity, to become more vulnerable yourself. To recognize our common humanity. To recognize the sacredness of our lives. Teresa offers us this gift, and it's one to be received with respect and gratitude.

Dinah Simmons

Author of *Mary Magdalene, Apostle to the Apostles*

www.ingramcontent.com/pod-product-compliance
Lightning Source LLC
LaVergne TN
LVHW050625090426
835512LV00007B/670